Manland

Manland

Peter Raynard

Nine
Arches
Press

Manland
Peter Raynard

ISBN: 978-1-913437-40-4
eISBN: 978-1-913437-41-1

First published July 2022 by:

Nine Arches Press
Unit 14, Sir Frank Whittle Business Centre,
Great Central Way, Rugby.
CV21 3XH
United Kingdom

www.ninearchespress.com

Printed in the United Kingdom by:
Imprint Digital

Nine Arches Press is supported using public funding by Arts Council England.

Supported using public funding by
**ARTS COUNCIL
ENGLAND**

Contents

Maelstrom

The murmuration of men takes on man-sized issues.
At issue (bless you) is the mendacious belief by the many
men of menace perched in their man-cave menageries
that male 'issues' can be mended by menfolk.   Aldermen

with their crunching admen's abdomens say mankind
is in danger. Save the Male is manifold.   They mention
the manscape doesn't need mansplaining.   But what about
the many man-sexuals made mental when caught unmanned?

No menu mentions the role played by the men in black
big blonde Bond men monumental mentors playing
a mendicant role with tremendous malevolence
on the manors of other men.   This is bad manners.

We men must look to the phenomenal manpower
found with menthol men, men with men, so be a mensch
throw off your manacles, open your mandibles
turn man upside down, and sing men men men men

manly men, men, men, oo hoo hoo, hooo, oo, oo, oo, oo hoo....

What the Older Men Tell Each Other about their Depression

Tall Man Syndrome

"I wish I was a little bit taller I wish I was a baller
I wish I had a girl who looked good I would call her" – Skee-Lo

Caesar geezer / guv bruv cus / bomb-drop pecs /
wink blink tight / fragrant flaunt / flagrant height /
photoshop app / handsome chap / cobblestone pack
/ kids on his sleeve / man-about-the-house / life's a
heave / reps steps / push up pull up / provider the
measure / the pressure / keep it all in / hands down
fiction / write lines on palms / genetic scars / across
acres of land / the fistful sound / of fitful screams /
weakness at the knees / wet face wobble / 24 hours /
taste so sour / love's lost strength / fossil fuel powered
/ no stone-faced coward.

Go On My Son

No-one you serve knows how you lost
your final years as a teenager staring
into the eyes of a suicide. Years without
formal education, now you are working
cutting shaping replacing keys shoes
phones watches for the privileged
of the town on a floorboard wage.

Your hands are now man's hands collecting
black cuts turning to red scars
from the cutting shaping replacing.
You are learning about people,
how they still see you as untested.
They can't know all that you learned
in a suspended life in dreams of your death.

We worked together, making each day
a passing thought, pitting it against
the next day, and the next, until
you were ready. Out the other side
with a world to learn cutting
and shaping a place for yourself
one key shoe phone watch at a time.

Home-Father Has Shit on the Carpet

Love is not a lump of shit on a white carpet
when the carpet is no longer white
when it can be no longer called a carpet
when there is only Calpol on a spoon
with a baby screaming into a room
with all of its contents now crammed inside
this Home-Father's head. He starts to question
the apocryphal power of such purple syrup.
Maybe baby is hungry. Home-Father needs a spliff.

He always wanted to do a philosophy degree
or an engineering degree or better still
a philosophy of engineering degree
that by degree would show him the mechanics
of a quiet world. He could do it in France,
they love theory. Now Home-Father thinks
he's shit himself. Will nobody help him?
He can't do this by himself in the middle
of the night when everyone is dead, refusing
to rise and all the others who now realise
we are put on this earth to wipe away
all of the shit we never shit in the first place
but are still meant to call it love. Shit!

The Fall

after Jonathan Glazer

the men, faces masked, look up
to the man who clings to the tree
rustle of sweet oak you know
the gloaming year
shouting shaking the tree
see the leaves shake him down

bark & dance there he lies
a shivering sin, gather round
kick & punch, stretch him
out, thumb his throat, smile
at the flash, snap/snap

snatch him up, noose his neck
the stench the hole below
the falling rope the hissing rope
the weight of the man
the smoking rope against the wood
its lash in the dark

look down at the gloom
the dark of the hole
ghost of the fall
the silence below
away they go

sly as soft rain
square light above
the glean of his face
the stretch of his legs
make steps of the hold
arms will not fold
as he goes

he climbs to the light
the men they go
he climbs to the light
the men they know
he climbs to the light
they think they know.
You know?

mano a mano

The man thinks he's being the reasonable man
as he holds me back, dishing out grief
with his son saying *'leave it dad, not again'*
a verbal stab into his dad's beliefs.

As he holds me back, dishing out grief
I try to assess how we got to this place
a solid stab driven into his lad's beliefs.
Language paralyses an already paralysed face

when trying to assess how we got to this place
something his son is well drilled in. Crazy
language paralyses an already paralysed face.
Under duress, violence is a marching army,

something his son is well drilled in. Crazy
to think all power lies in the mouth, not the soul.
Under duress, violence is a marching army
heading towards a constellation of inch-blood holes.

Thinking all power lies in the hand, not the soul
so a normal life can't be about me on a march
heading towards a constellation of inch-blood holes.
My moving hand becomes a fisted charge

so a normal life can't be about me on a march
trying to talk him down so I won't find
my moving hand becoming a fisted charge.
But a moving train is a moving mind

trying to talk him down so I can find
a way out, backing away so he can win this one.
But a moving train is a moving mind
with a thousand views pinging around my brain

to a way out, backing away, so that I win this one.
Like me, he lacked a mirrored angle, with an explosion
of a thousand views pinging around his brain.
And the man thought he was being the reasonable man.

Work-Father Weekends

Every weekend GoPro Work-Fathers wake at five a.m.
to build rail tracks car parks and paint blue stripes
across the top of A4 sheets with a yellow splotch of sun
as their children play with trains, dolls, and guns.

Newly born Work-Fathers, who baby their baby
in a front chest arrangement of ante-natal empathy
splatter the bitten high streets on the verge of collapse
scared shitless baby will wake needing the contents

of Home-Mother goodies to quieten the teat-beast within.
Home-Mothers are asleep or on Facebook posting
witty anecdotes about the uselessness of Work-Fathers
which makes them all secretly cry into their pillows.

They remember their mother saying, *'even when you're eighty
you'll never stop worrying about them'*, laying fallow
the brightly-coloured two-for-one offers on perfection
so all the wretched *etceteras* of life never matter again.

X Marks the Man

for Richard

For some older men   the *x* from a woman
after her name in a message
can still raise a smile   a lusty eyebrow maybe
misperception often flows freely from that gland.

We should praise the young men   who sign off
with an *x* to other male friends   fathers   brothers   cousins
as if some kind of newfound oath.
Not held back by the pantheon of past men   xxx

Home-Father is Given Testosterone

Never mind the year-round overheating
our Father is ready   like a cocked trigger
gun full of happy bullets   that globule
of junk gives   when injected into his buttock

each quarter   not having the jab comes with
long-term possibilities   heart disease
the main outcome   all of life is a series
of side effects   one action producing

a reaction   topping up an empty tank
flaccid drop for a man in late-middle age
but it's not a straightforward recipe
as it tends to boil over so he can't stop

thinking about sex   in bed   the shower
even the front room on a weekend.
every woman becomes a curvature
bringing him back to base   a smutty radar

carnal extruder   is this what man becomes?
Driver of a full-metal motor   veering
around on its own   everything arouses
the sun from a cloud   wild horses

on nomansland   but on the a.m. school run
with lycra-clad Mothers?   or at Tesco's?
With the cashiers in their alluring blue
uniforms   perfect control at the tills

even the security guy prompts a glint
there's no wisp of competition to all this
no   on your marks   ding-ding   (g)loved up
in the ring   but it's all a bit too much

when it accumulates in the mind at a time
when things need doing   don't believe him?
you try cooking dinner with a hard on   no man
can think about food   carrying such a burden.

Violence Decides

'Poverty is the worst form of violence.' – Gandhi

Violence reads the autocue with a lobotomised look   a
curled lip creased amongst a thicket of words   Violence
has a black belt in tunnel vision where on various
birthdays   christenings weddings   he is violence-in-
waiting silently observing the direction dialectics of a
drunken dispute.   Lord Almighty Violence is in his
pulpit sharing the bread of unwavering damnation
with a massage of stygian facts   obscuring the
evangelical roadside placards   extolling Violent body
parts   passing judgement day on dead soldiers same-
sex brothers and sisters   druggie drop-outs from the
impoverishment of a blank sheet.   Violence draws
up a personal independence plan   for the alcoholic
so soaked it gets him a job behind the bar as an optic.
Violence is the Order Paper pointing questions towards
an obfuscation of meetings   greetings and beatings.
Violence does the doorsteps canvassing your cheeks to
see which way you blanch.   For there will ever be some
wastrel   jack-booting an arm in his mother's basement
to a *Valkyrie* soundtrack.

Bald Truth

There is a brown curtain in the corner
of the barbers and a large glass tank
at the end of a row of plastic chairs.

Two fat pythons lie inside, roped together
in slumber. Two fat barbers, leather aprons,
buzz away at the necks of their young victims

as I wait with my Dad to have my own head
readied for the posh school. *Next!* A flat capped
man stands, shuffles behind the curtain.

I hear quiet murmurings, clipped snippets
of conversation. The owner, a man
of many stripes unties the snakes hauling one

around my neck. It is warm silky calm graceful
in its slow-motion weight. Smooth as the top

of my head now.   The man behind the curtain
returns, smiles at me wearing the snake, says

'nice scarf'. Leaves with a head of hair snug
as a helmet, the best a dying man can get.

Careers Day for Home-Father

for Cathy

Home-Father and three Work-Mothers go to show
little children at school what to do when they grow up
and make enough money to stop their own
inevitable children dying from digital malnutrition.

One mother is an actuary actually so can predict the future
but the way the world is so certain to end she won't win.
Not that it's a competition, Home-Father assures himself,
holding a plate of homemade chocolate-chip cupcakes

in his rubbery yellow hands. His wife is a Green.
She can see the earth is going to shit so the children
must recycle cardboard and not eat plastic to stop life
coming to a roaring end. She'll come last. On arrival

Home-Father spots an opera-singing Father
dominating the acoustics of the school's corridors.
This annoys him no end as it deflects the children's
attention away from his brilliant solar-power-point

presentation on the value of time management
in & out shake it all about in the home. The kids love
the cupcakes and enjoy blowing up the Marigold gloves,
bouncing them off each other's heads. He watches them

do what they're not meant to be doing, knowing
it's exactly what they should be doing at such an age.
He's lost even though he knows it's not a game,
not when you've nothing to show for your troubles.

Animal Cruelty

CUT   into the quotidian playground bully ritual of
what's it to be? head-butt kick in the balls or a good
old-fashioned punch to the jaw. Can I have a head-
butt please? I already have a thump, thump, thumping
whistle blows CUT glass gun bottle boot fist
knife   chain   language boys   choices, choices step
right up   everyone's a lottery sinner   CUT   it has to
be said   it's just whether there's words to say it   CUT
violence as body language   as direction   solution.
Understand?   An allusion do you feel plucky skunk
in the dim light of this intimate delusion   CUT   wall
outside the pub   line of ducks   quack quack quack
with the crack pints spliffs open doors sharp parked
car   cowl-browed man steps out   one arm hanging
like a noose   lifts the gun   shot to the head   prizes
prizes   *close enough to watch his brains flow by*/ Bye
CUT   everyone minding their own   indolent witness
sees a neck to a glass jugular flows pinched neck by
a man who makes it his business   fingers slip their
grip from blood   still saves a life   a single breath of
success CUT for the greater good angels always had
defaced faces   violence filled the gasps   the required
intensity for breathing CUT CUT CUT CUT CUT
to an unending reel of parents   sat in silence   ticking
off each absent night since their boy bought a bargain
in a marketplace fight.

On Hearing Racist Chants at a Steel Pulse Gig

Tiffany's, Coventry 1977

I stop walking on the spot, fifteen-year-old
petrified punk   soap-spiked hair

no holler & ball to shoulder blade them all.
Shaming my city of peace once blitzed

by the Nazis. Skinny little white boy
I wish violence was my intention   one racist

the less the better the show   too scared
to be a good Samaritan to the lyric.

Now I fight back the fight in me   to rage
against white man minstrels   medieval tongues

lashing at the English language   jongleurs of hate
setting it ablaze in monosyllabic time. History

their palingenetic fault line   precious
as a cobweb. Rub a dub dub   drum & bass thud

keeping time to beat down Babylon
beat down working-class feet jackboot Johnnies

disgracing granddad Tommies who we mark
for the march they took   so gimme a gimme

a gimme a   festival of hope   for most
of us arrived here by plane or boat.

Home-Father Hydraulics

Carrying a bag of Tesco's finest, Home-Father
sees a crowd watching an attack on a homeless person
smattering the air with *'leave him alone'*.

Our Father rams his shoulder into the attacker's ribs.
The air leaves them. They roll together
the man unsure of our shopper's intent,

Home-Father hopeful of instilling some sense.
The attacker looks at the bag of goods
littering the litter, then at Home-Father's

pallid face as if knowing his action was done
as much for him as his victim. The attacker
ambles off, his victim too. People hand out

their *'well-done'*. Home-Father enjoyed
the rushing reality of the fight, being kicked
in the equilibrium, out of breath, for once

seeing onlookers feel the sanctity of shame,
scanning the credits for their names.

You Talking to Me?

*'The whole problem with the world is that fools and fanatics are always so
certain of themselves, and wiser people so full of doubts.' – Bertrand Russell*

Discussion unfolds like a front-page scoop
that knits the purl of a bloody dispute.

In the fruit bowl of cups of tea, couple of pints,
breaking bread, sat at a table, on your knees

nose-to-nose problems arise when unused
to another's game play. Such noise also flows

under arrogant bridges spanning two richly
educated rivers where the *'they'* in *'they said'*

is oracle, bulleted with *'nothing of the kind'*
& *'puh-leeze'* – privileged weapons against empathy

until you're told to wipe that political position
off your working-class rowing boat. Full stops

include: *'it's always been a one-way street as far
as I'm concerned.'* or *'I don't care what you say*

about smoking, my nan lived till she was ninety'.
If all else fails to persuade, there's always the *'but still'*

the fine detail trump-of-all-cards not to be played
too early for fear of an undisputed spat that lets

the lions loose in your own den of antiquity. But still
if none of such floats your throat there's always

the dulcet twist to be found in the space between
what you believe, what you say, and what the fuck

you are going to do about it. Now, who wants a fight?

Home-Father's First After School Play Date

The ticks are clocking, expectations flat
even the moon's got enough on its plate.
Battered food lies impatient in the freezer,
sugar-free juices, salty snacks, nuts? No sir!

Home-Mothers' numbers typed into I.C.E.
Planned with conciliatory precision
– 'free play' – a boardgame nobody wins,
some drawing, food, then a strictly observed
half-hour of mildly educational TV.

Sixty seconds in, control is lost, blurred lines
of 'play fight/real fight' – shouts from the garden
'let's turn on the hedge trimmer' as Home-Father
has his head in the oven. Trust is a foolish
parent's timebomb. Home-Mothers return

scoop up loved ones, move on: other siblings
are to be picked up, there's evening classes,
PTA later, and a flagon of grapes await.
Home-Father scans the blitzkrieg of collateral
damage, thankful the house is back in allied hands.

The Great Depression

At these times they walk around at night
with a baseball bat hoping they will lose
before they all fall to the chaos of this world

fearful of withdrawing from themselves.
With an anger of another's concoction
at these times they walk around at night

hunting for dotted-knuckled bulbous bruisers
tracers of cornered school-ground violence
before they all fall to the chaos of this world.

Looking for first dibs on a bag of thrills
graduation day is near for these fellas.
At these times they walk around at night

careful to grab their own crap and frown. Easy
as swinging a cat by its tail between walls
before they all fall to the chaos of this world.

Dampen your own fire   for you never dare look
where the gap in any man's teeth leads to
for at these times they walk around at night
before they all fall to the chaos of this world.

My Dick is more Sexist than your Dick

after Salena Godden

My dick is an absent father never done the dishes nor changed a nappy dick
My dick is Testosterone Wrecks, always on top, head of the queue dick
My dick is a come and have a go if you think you're hard enough dick
My dick is more sexist than your dick

My dick is an Aryan, Proud Boy, Oath Keeping dick
My dick is rocket man in your pocket man nuclear arsenal dick
My dick chairs the UN Commission for Women's Rights dick
My dick is more sexist than your dick

My dick is a builder's arse, suited and booted, superhero dick
My dick is a dick pic, thick slick flick-of-the-wrist rope-trick dick
My dick invented Viagra to secure a super race of dicks
My dick is more sexist than your dick

My dick is a casting couch you play the part dick
My dick is an unreported, didn't go to trial, rape joke dick
My dick is a TV serial killer, a girl found in the woods novel dick
My dick is more sexist than your dick.

these boys

JONNY – we used to drive him mad playing with his locks
in Year 8 computer science, began coding in juniors,
quiet like but you knew when he was in any room – TED
         – straight arms, wrists handled behind his back,
             a lean-to of *'shit or bust'* – laid out
         on the table like a victim – his own worst enemy
            doesn't even cover the body – CHARLIE –
had a skateboard stuck to his feet –
life was a grinding rail – never said why
he was in care – why he couldn't stay in one place –
everyone has some kind of darkness
but he had nothing but – MICKY – grew so tall
            must have been raised in a greenhouse,
         could drop a three-point basket sitting down
         boy could he fly, can still feel the breeze of him
         hear it too always chatting some kind of shit
usually about some girl – BEN – got the weed off his big brother –
bottom of the frosted fields lunchtime,
cold air hiding our smoke – totally licked
for session 5, still don't know how
we got away with it – i guess he didn't – JACOB –
         turned right up high on repeat, probably addicted
to Teletubbies in a previous life, wanted everything again/again –
         first week of university must be a mad thing, more
         of the more, knocking down your door – in English
         he'd sometimes say, *'who gives a fuck what the dead think'* –
must have got curious though, because he fucking knows now –
no-one wants to know the definition of an epidemic –
the put upon of people – everyone knows someone –
everyone flicks through the channels
of their supersized packages unable to watch
the morphine dance – teachers count the A graders –
count the graduates – count their dwindled coffers –

they count the absences of these boys –
these boys left hanging over their homework –
these boys hiding in the woods (always the woods) –
these boys given to impetuous –
these boys who now sit round the big table upstairs
their lips sewn together by the expectation
thinking   what   the   fuck   did   you   expect?

Home-Father is Entrusted with
the Mysteries of Everyday Life

Even after the hunter gathering
OCD cleaning, dropping off/picking up
head-to-toe healthcare appointments
great swathes of the day lay unsown.

During such time gaps Home-Father
often sparks up   watches a *Loose Women*
debate on weekend celibacy. He could embark
on some DIY but that would break

the Home-Mothers' omertà, causing
the Work-Fathers to ask why their wives
can't touch up the skirting with a lick
of emulsion. Home-Father doesn't want

to get stuck into that mouldy old bag
of onions harvested from the allotment.
Not at a time of great global fluidity
that sees Work-Mothers on the rise.

Yet still feeling a little sick by the fact
they could never envision the tectonic change
children bring. Why   together they didn't
sit down draw up a plan   find an app

or AI device to calibrate the historically
troubled question: How do we stop
the tiny twig we found in the woods
being thrown against life's wall?

I never taught my sons how to fight

with a clenched fist   in front of a worried brow
one foot forward   a trembling calf   trying
not to get in the way of yourself   it's a dance
not a mime   you're looking straight and through
an eye   lash   chin touching chest   incoming
shoulder   knuckles a gnarl   it's more than
a defence   comes with a sell by date
don't think how another will react   get it
all out   bleed the mind   drive the hand on   pause
look back at what you have done   you'll see
where you went wrong   but don't mistake this
as some late ring session   on how to fight   read
it more   as life's long lesson   on how to write.

The Field at the End of Our Road

that's us   jumping brooks
tell your mum I saved you

that's us   with a knife cutting up
that dead rabbit   fieldwork biology

remember the horses ran amuck
when I blew my trumpet?
made the farmer mad as fuck

that's us   taking tadpoles home
jumping frogs in our gardens

that's us   playing war   throwing
grenades of horse manure

that's us   smoking weed, dropping
mushrooms   watching sheep dance
the cows getting all moody   remember

when they found that young lad by the pond?
we never went back down for so so long.

Home-Father's School Daze

Plagued with elegance, Home-Mothers arrive en-masse
recounting midday errands, after-school plans.

Sleep-filled Bengali Fathers have risen
to pick up their kids before heading out

to deposit various people in various states
of inebriation across various places of this earth.

A couple of Grand-Fathers in tow with 'her indoors'
complete the human presence.   Pigeons and crows

have their forensic moment in the playground still.
Everything is primary now; fun gives way

underfoot to tarmac foam, speckled with stars
lines to a child's future.

Home-Father searches for his own time
of grazed knees and elbows, latched on

to the metal climbing frame
dressed up with limpet kids.

An open door signals school's end
birds fly off to their airborne canvas.

Home-Father remembers running
towards his own Mother with a flock

of hunger beside him   chirping   singing
the only pure echoes of his past.

A Sestina to Die For

You know the way this goes by now
days wending their way, stretching out
the last drop-down-menu of clarity
filling out the self-referral form when applying
for the post of interviewee. Name, age, address
of your conditions, no option for a blank face.

You carry on, nearly finished? Can you face
your family and friends? Is life better now
you have realised your mistakes? Is your address
still the same? How often do you go out?
How many jobs have you been applying
for lately? You cannot clear the fog without clarity.

There are no wrong answers, though a degree of clarity
is required with the digital triage you will face
so take time to revise due diligence when applying
yourself.   We thought you would be well by now.
Are you finding the process impossible to work out?
You may want to drop in at this address.

We understand if you feel it is wrong to address
you this way so one last time for clarity
for we have a responsibility to get referrals out
of the system before we can let in a new face.
This is your final warning, are you listening? Now
some loss adjustment to your fate is worth applying

your attention to in the jobs you will be applying
for in the coming weeks. You must find an address
that is a permanent option. How long has it now
been since you decided to be disabled? Wow such clarity
in your answer, we're getting somewhere finally. Face
the front please, you know I can't help you out

if you're not willing to stay alive. Are you often out
lukewarm on the sofa with the telly on? I'm applying
a great deal of patience to my pro-forma, it's time to face
facts. This mime act must end. The methadone will address
the rough edges of this mess with a precision and clarity
that will help bring you back to the here and now.

Family and friends there is no reply at his address
we wondered if you could give us some clarity
as you can appreciate we need all of this to end now.

Home-Father's Beside Himself at the Seaside

Besides the driver who has the face of a child killer,
Home-Father is the only man on the trip.
All the Year 3s still call him Miss.

The bundles of green jumpers are so excited,
many have never seen the sea in real life before.
'How does the sea make waves Miss?' they shout at him.

He tells them it depends on the moon's mood
which makes the children run into the crashing
white curls fully-uniformed before Head Teacher's

voice freeze-frames the scene. The children stand
like a Gormley exhibition as she pulls out a long rope,
gives one end to Home-Father and they walk barefoot

into the sea. He now knows the meaning of a lifeline
as no children are allowed past the rope else the moon
will make sure the tides and waves stop them

from ever going home. This is more like it, he thinks
for this is strong work. He looks along the rope
at Head Teacher, her arched back, arms straight.

He's totally entranced by the control conjured up
by someone whose tiny shiny black loafers
now bob imperiously towards them
like a pair of obedient puppies.

SWIMMING AWAY IN CIRCLES

Drugs Research with Ground Floor Experience

Recruiting Interviewees

The tenth-floor corridors would make Kafka chuck
his book against death-row doors   some barred up
all painted an even hue. Deposits at doorways
out-of-work boots   dog bowl   pot of failing flowers

ghost of roses. Echoes from within   parrot squawks
whistling kettle   feet thump across a lino floor
plates clap their way out of washing bowls   tombola
of shouts   laughs   songs *I remember you, you arsehole*.

'Come on down   don't hesitate £10 cash to partake'
We post leaflets about our research   taking their place
with kaleidoscopic delight   for hungry house hoarders
all-you-can't-afford credit cards   loan shark side-orders.

We retreat to our interview room   cup of tea a smoke
the dim wait for people   under skylines that are broke.

1. The Redundant

Size of a planet hunkers in his seat   head mark
a sunken sandpit adult's fontanelle   a stark
recap of a crash unhidden by stubborn strands
still sweeps a comb through. Fingers ley line bands

on his palm   always with spirits on his lip
that bring him to this psychiatric lucky dip.
He has no teeth on show   barbarian breath
at the back of his throat the malignant spread

of days dried up in his king-size metastasis
preparing the dam of everyday dependence
the universal flood of articulated booze
snorting more lines than given at school.

Slings a trebuchet of words, his grand finale
'I'm nothing special, now give me my money'.

2. The Homeless Boys

Double act of heroin   in the present tense
twinned by free-range parental inheritance
smell of the street   two faces both bloody
best not think   what they'll do for the money.

Gimlet eyes loll skywards   as if to look inside.
Boy one the wayfarer   thin as his grin   white
as expectant powder   takes him well beyond high.
Boy two's the talker   a market trader of words

back of the van   a gift for the garbage of their day
crisp sandwich of monotony   focused on the way
he deals with questions   like a crooked croupier
who sweeps up the cards and chips for the camera.

Money's the object   but not for the right reasons
answers swell chests   with a skill for all seasons.

3. *The Soldier*

There are scrapes of red   like paint on his face
his palms stuck close to his jaw   fingers crawling
against his cheeks   keeping the past lingering
across a skewed line of vision. A pause   he speaks

of followers who watch him   as he dances
to a playlist of pain. Self-harm sees a spike
in attention   as they take a festering glance.
Table judders to restless legs. Not much to write

about illegal drugs. Dabbled socially thanks
backfired attempts   to be like the rest   be normal
by putting out a fire   with your bare feet. He stamps
at the moment sees this as a test   a formal

report he'll pass only if he's erred   strayed
distraught at the thought   that he won't be paid.

4. The Widow

Tattooed lady   retired from her phantom circus
fag long as a dinosaur's claw   holds perilous
ash over open palm. Rat-sized mutt tied to the table.
Her eyes a bluer shade of tomb   with a bible

brow she answers questions through a history of lips.
Paints a husband long gone to a hit and miss
self-serving checkout kiss. No use for her magic wand
that took her back to the blitz and the bombs

underground shelters   *Just a minute dear,* up she rises
makes her way to the entrance   pauses in spaces
between what she came for and what she brought.
Like automatic doors frozen by thoughts

she never meant to see again. Manages to clear the fog
of memories   leaves without the money or her dog.

5. *The Mariner*

He holds no store of sunken ships   kept sail
with arms as strong as an anchor. Tattoos
are *de rigeur*   just like his salty ways.
As if he was born with wooden toes

he dances a glance between harmless chairs
swinging away at a windless room laid bare
with only land in sight. He gives a cold hard stare
as he takes to telling his tales   then swears

that if any man wants a fight with him
he'll be having a fag outside. But wait
I say   what about the questionnaire   now grim
teeth bare through frazzled beard   with great

big heave   he blows all of the papers to curl
up in dread as he shouts: *'you calling me a girl?'*

6. The Mother's Ghost

Line after line after line   streak her arms.
Crossed fingers   nibbled nails   close to break
like bowline knots   in a storm of harm
cracked teeth   she knows what's at stake

led around like a rabid puppy filled with disgust
at the medicated feats   of a doctor's cost.
What can you say   to a young woman lost
whose life was never sprinkled   with fairy dust.

I should start   but she keeps staring across
at her shiny floor Mother   who's at a loss
to find answers to her past   all the forgiving
fixing the fittings of her daughter. Leaving

with the tenner & blank questionnaire   which I fill
out with a mother's wish   she was her child still.

7. *The Boxer*

A life on the buildings and work in the ring
face full of muscle   knuckles that sing
a tale of two pities   fingers drum tap
message of displeasure   answers a slap

of bad practice days   drenched in the gym.
A belt from your dad   not worth the fight
long-coat at the door   won't let you in
home to a bottle   when will it go right?

Cracks the bone of a question   guile heavy jab.
In the pub he sees the fading fealty
of people to the state   no land to grab
no grace in a church   without a pure deity.

He's run out of time   the form is still blank
up from his corner   no time to fight back.

8. The City Worker

What can you do   when there's no-one to thank
for all your brass honesty   fuelled by the speed
of coke and eez   drug mulch swim   in a septic tank
of a city centre gastro   where people eat greed.

Brash as the all-day Sunday lash   an antidote
after the dollar/dollar   a mid-week cheeky
melee   Saturday's excess   Monday's big smoke.
White stick smile   sees the light of Friday fully

suited   plush-stained packet of bills   mentions
ventures the capital has no need for. He could
go on   about thirty-something corruptions
but I've run out of questions   says he should

up tricks   but bowls me a full toss look to score
'what the fuck do you want to do this shit for?'

9. The Disabled Man

Blister pack of stimulation   life is a septic in-growing toenail
nightly bowls of cornflakes and weed   heady cocktail

helps the medicine go down   to sleep away autoimmunity
up for coffee   then the bog for Charlie   the daily spree

a tightrope lined   with pills for accepted conditions
where balance is more of a whim than an act. An exhibition

of over and out   from the side and below   this man sits
at the depth of times   waiting on a change that spits

on you from a devastating height of hope. Hunger
is an ever present fickle companion   a stubborn lung

refusing to breathe. Fast forward   to this place   this seat
and you have the face of an island   sick of the sea.

10. The Student

Twenty-thousand leagues out my depth   lad lands
with a face like a suicide note of failed demands

wedged in the sixth-form curriculum   from ten
GCSEs to University   the next birthing channel when

no-one thinks to ask why. A lineage to learn
found under the skin   keep going   till you feel the burn.

Pass that black cap & gown   you never get to keep
who the hell knows   when to make the leap

to forgo faith in such finality. Choice choices. What
can't I do for you today? This is not a wrong turn   stop

the crystal ball. Subjects aren't the problem   it's the game
they want you to play   serving the sham architects of Cain.

I can give you the tenner   a number to call
it's easy to forget   what your fingers are for.

The Findings

The results are in   dear ladies and gents
the news is confused   what did you expect

that the redundant man   with a hole in his head
was wrong in saying   he was just like the rest

what would you do   with Boy One & Boy Two
whacked out on smack   well beyond school

the grunt   who scrapes away at his face
sick of being told   to stay in his place

the painted old widow   who's doing no harm
left with the memory   of being infirm

the sea dog who's feet   have run aground
now just wants someone   to give him a hand

the young woman   all tagged up with blame
a mother gone mad   with worry and shame

the boxer   the builder   the heaviest drinker
seeking relief   in cheap cans of cider

the city worker   such honest corruption
counters the fever   with pills of disruption

the disabled capsule's   catatonic normality
floats his ocean biology   redefining reality

a teenage boy   someone else's ambition;
a teacher a parent   stand over his coffin.

this census of people   told all is commercial
hear Kafka laugh   as they swim away in circles.

Nothing to Report

The walk in the bright baleful sun.

Just the ticket
to the platform   meeting a friend?

The metal tracks protected
behind yellow lines
waiting with the rest
at the end   a soft green sign

its nudging words *'we're in your corner'*
'talk to us'
a flush of thoughts
a tickety-tack   the click of the tracks

tunnelling wind
the roar of the train

emerging fierce
wincing face   in the blinding shine

the blur of a driver   who can't stop.
But can a man stop so late on?   Can he not

sit and wait to hear the sound
of others calling him back?

This man can.

Home-Father's Half-Term Teenagers

Ha! No, no, it's fine all under control, the boys
are over the what's that/why's that less
put that down/pick that up/turn that off
hold on no you can't/sit up straight/get dressed.

Words lie dormant on a shelf of inky memories.
You see, it's more a wherefore art thou, out now
on their own, rabbits running across fields parks
through the fence top of the school roof no sense

of time it's fine they've done all that keeping up
hardly noticing the day as night backwards
forwards one long fluid progression towards
independence day. Yes, yes I am getting old

but you never forget how to push a chair
around the streets, bent over a grand one
from your own. Though used as a threat foretold
revenge is never a dish best served old. Now hop it!

A Sky Blue Glosa

for Cov

We love you city, we do
We love you city, we do
We love you city, we do
Oh, City we love you!

After a week or a year indoors
I go out with my son for a walk
faces masked like ultras, down
the middle of the road we go.
Free from traffic we're reminded
of match days walking the streets
chanting our song on repeat
with an inflated rush of nerves
rising from beery breaths.
We love you City, we do!

Thump of our feet marching
with non-violent intent.
People on doorsteps,
with stubborn elbows
and high pitched ears,
have heard it all before.
We love you City, we do!

And those forever dying
remember when home
was a target – labelled
like luggage they left
the city for the safety of fields.
They know the score.
It's so we can sing
We love you City, we do!

Today we're united,
practising the art of inaction
keeping inside locked up tight
to save a life. Reduced
to watching memories
through our windows.
Along the white line we go
singing in our heads
Oh, City we love you!

Tributes at the Golden Gate Bridge

The early mist that hovered
like a veil of mourning
under the bridge is lost.

As we watch the wind whip
white curls across the water
my friend says to me
with desert dry wit

*'people come from all over the world
to jump from this bridge'*

Across at Crissy Field
1,300 pairs of footwear
are laid out in rows:

front & centre a brace
of WW1 boots, puttees intact
stand to attention
beside limp green flip-flops.
The first, next to the latest to be found.

Footsteps stretch back
to the bay and the bridge
where each foot stood.

So soft to touch at the shore
from a 220ft drop
hard as a sculpture.

Home-Father Blames the Work-Fathers

It's not all Sky Sports News and masturbation
often it's cleaning and shopping to sustain

his three-bar family. But on his first real run
start of term he hears a: *'Hello Home-Father,'*

from a PTA Home-Mother, sharp as raw garlic
taking him from behind at the tills. *'Is Work-Mother ill?'*

she asks, looking at his trolley of well-meaning
mix of good and evil. *'Oh I forgot, she can't drive'*

she says. Perceiving misandry, Home-Father never thought
he was the type of *man* most forthright in spreading

his truth so thickly on a Mother's Pride slice of point-blank
petulance. Recovering in his car he seethes at the image

of him firing a white noise response right between
the guise of said PTA/Home-Mother. *'Home-Parenting*

is not all Sky Sports News and masturbation you know.'
'Isn't it? She jabbed, *'I must be doing it wrong then.'*

Something for the Pain

Under a forest canopy, soprano bats eat
in the dirt of daytime, feasting freely

on the buzz of crunchy Diptera, cheating
the conspiracy of leaves above where daylight

flutters on, choking from our growth.

From this darkness he draws a glow
from a glass pipe, crackling grass the flow

of welcome anxieties, a chest full of trees
exhaling endless impossibilities.

Home-Father Doubts the Doubts

Hood up with a mug of coffee the size of a potty
Home-Father isn't watching the TV's grey stares.
The long-tailed morning is a rattle that didn't shake
and the three-hour time trial lays in wait.
No-one is there to paint this image of a man
at work with his tasks freeze-framed about the house.

A Home-Mother once went on strike in dispute
with her no-pay offspring who assumed
the earth turned like a remote-controlled roll mop.
Clothes piled upon pile, dishes high as a roman orgy
bathroom a no-go area except for pubic curlicues
guarding the toilet bowl as though impatient

for a born-again christening. She was a patient
stalwartean Home-Mother who took a stand
for all others by doing nothing, until a natured urge
forced her hand into the clothes, the dishes,
the toilet bowl, into the unending tide of powder,
liquid, spray, brush, vacuum, enough to give anybody

an extreme political view of life. Home-Father
was patient also, but his was egged on
by the impressive inertia of depression
in a world rummaging around for precision
instead of celebrating the glorious mess of it all.

Rabbie

For my Father, life has ever been
a *braw bricht moonlit nicht* –
but Lauder was no Burns
for the Ayrshire Bard's picture
was a fixture on the shelf
within a line of our kin.
Though my Father never read poetry
Burns was the man
like Celtic the team
pints of heavy or whisky the drinks
leaving Scotland the means
to go down South
behind auld enemy lines
armed with saltire crosses
their brogue voices lilting
the bars with songs
for the displaced who
wandered many a weary foot
singing their way home
for the sake of a fading time
for the sake of Auld Lang Syne.

Redefining Progress

The land man's drone hovers over his slavering selection
of pigs before their poke. The trough is a circle of pink arses
like a ring of buffet prawns, snuffling at the feed, the filth
of mud-stuck trotters in a competition of grunts & steam.

A new pig wedges his pale pink difference between the main
hog and its lieutenant. Noshes on, keeping his metal truck
stomach up with appearances. He cannot be certain of timings,
snaffles the pellets of protein down his constricted gullet.

The consumption is furious in its disgust, in its fear of an ending.
On and on, this revolution of fattening, this group, this round,
feeding themselves towards their own St Martin's day menu
of tongue, cheek, belly, loin, rasher, chop, chop, chop, filling

this bulging craven earth with its burning bowels splashing
onto cracked heels as we eat from the palm of opulent fiction.

the length of a lie > the length of a truth

When my son's fingers matched his years
I told him I once believed I was dead –
a condition known as Cotard Syndrome.
'What? Dead/dead, amongst the living?
Like Michael Jackson in Thriller? Or the film
we watched the other day, Zombieland?
Did you look like a Zombie, flaky faced?'

I don't tell him it was more like being
a bug-eyed ghost in quicksand, in Batman
pyjamas my illness had stopped me growing
out of, watching other kids troop up to school.

Face like an excited orphan, he says, 'Cotard Syndrome?
Did you ever think you could live forever being dead?'
I don't tell him the world went in one eye and came out the other.
'Will you teach me how to be dead?' After school, maybe.

He leaves me at the gates trailing his rucksack
wondering if such a badass trait is hereditary.
Missing a handful of years he saw the certainty
of death as a big number so was dying
to tell his friends about his dead dad.
I've never told him death is a single figure
even though an uncertain lie takes longer
to tell than any dead certain truth.

Acceptance Ghazal

I use this form to flirt about ill-health, tell you I'm disabled
though you won't hear the stricken deer, I am disabled.

My nose can look round corners, my cheek adorns a scar
I juggle pairs of glasses but can't see very far, I am disabled

My drive to learn is a strong young bull charging
against a somatic glare, I am disabled.

I keep to daylight hours as much as my mind allows,
a long fight lost to fear, I am disabled

Watch out, I'll let you down when
saying that I'll be there, I am disabled

I'm a merry-go-round of syndromes,
with many tickets to spare, I am disabled

This is me, Peter Frank Raynard, an open-mouthed man –
looking back the view was always clear, I am disabled!

Being Disabled Takes Practice

So is it the usual kind?   much easier if it's the usual kind
       unless the usual kind
is not quite the same as it usually is   each kind can be made unusual
      if you find yourself

in an unusual environment   one that you may not be able to cope
      with   in the usual way
such as when you are at work   I know I know you can't work   but
     let's say the usual kind

is not unusual enough to forego the opportunity to work   now at work
     there will be
a number of unusual factors at play   that make your usual state
    of being   less usual

in terms of the way in which you would usually be able to cope   with
     your usual conditions.
I know it is hard to imagine   given your usual state of being
     but in such an unusual

situation   that would be a cause for concern   wouldn't it?
    that is something we usually could do something about
       such as sign you off work

for a period of time   but you insist
     it is the usual kind?
in the usual situation?   I know   that is what you
    usually say.   Oh well then

as I usually tell you   there isn't much I can do for you
I'm afraid   as you well know we've tried all the usual remedies
and some of the not so usual ones   and nothing

really worked. But if your condition does become unusual in any
way,   particularly if you are in an unusual situation   then you
know that I can be usually quite useful   see me again
in four weeks   if you can get an appointment
            close the door   on your way out.

Home-Father: A King in Waiting

The Waits began at birth, tiny yellow body six days
in neo-natal, comings and goings as we remained still

as if to move would see you disappear in our absence.
A&E, the go-to line when you were new to breathing.

Heaney's *Death of a Naturalist* stuck in the glove box
is beyond memory, as for Descartes, well I've done enough

thinking for one wait, in a car I had to keep ticking over
to keep warm. Snow white field, a risky adventure

looking back, how we let you camp on a winter's night
shows up the decisions we made to assuage your depression.

The pain-in-the-arse first gigs where the encore taunted us
coat-stand parents. Just finishing on the Xbox before a trip

to the gramps where you jumped in the car with no shoes.
Outside the last day at college, coaxing you to get the jab

Bob Marley's *I'm Still Waiting* on repeat. Like the old soak
Charles, I have waited too long, time to hand me my crown.

The Afterwards

In the afterwards there is only hard math
parents walking away hands full of death
young boys counting each dark moment
for those who keep the past on a thread
wound round fingers like waxed string
long enough to hang an ignorant throat.
Flushed with high-grade mouthwash we sing
into the afters with its ticking politic whilst
'we now go live' to a journalist arrested
as the inner city toasts its disapproval
at another blue murder struck by rusty years
of static power the germinal social distance
that pushes deaths into closed files.
Still expected to pick ourselves up
in the same backyard we lick our wounds
with burning tongues at a standing start
reaching out for a quiet rest where hope
is line of *big* men long gone. In the afterwards
lessons are measured by the time it takes
to calm a man down. Time enough to die.

We're the last now, for sure

Fluent in slur we curdled our fathers' ways
drinking dark pints on wet nights deep down
amongst the weeds. Many have fallen. Nigels
especially are on the wane, surpassed by Lucifer

but there are still those who keep going back
to the Edwards Harrys Williams. Still beguiled
by the posh consonants & foul vowels
of a gout riddled history, still keeping Eton alive.

We were the non-employed black-eyed boys,
a perennial brotherhood of gang fights, our salute
to the present times. Our grandparents died
when we were young as we breached the fast food

frontiers, left in the care of priests, teachers, coaches
all hiding in brash sight. We weren't brought up
with the glean of a screen where everything is free.
We owned boredom instead until Elvis left the pot.

The lucky 77s blending the rum of reggae with punk.
But we still held evolution's flame lighting up
our parent's gaze with shiny new lines.
The young have thrown away their wands –

they hold the wild reins now, sailing across a world
drenched in postmodern idolatry. The big men
threw acid in the eyes of science, as we sat
in the cheap seats tapping away at hotmail.com.

At Some Arthur's Round Table

How's your flow? asks Arthur, head
of a heat-filled round. As other knights fidget
with their grins. The quiet one remembers

when it sounded like a back yard tap
filling a watering can
with enough force to flatten grass.

He hears his sons pissing in the bowl
with abandon, strong as a horse
on a steaming sunlit morning.

'*It's all about one's aim these days*'
pipes up a brave knight withdrawing
yellowed fingers from a smoky mouth – *stop/*

start – control has gone like most other parts – Aye!
they cry. One man can't lift an eyelid,
most can't lift a smile. The quiet one's turn

to speak will come but he doesn't have
the balls to tell them in these late days
he sits down to piss like a woman

trying not to tear at the fear
of what may grow within.

See the Old Men Make their Exit

'shun! In unforgiving battles   fielding the flag
muscled silage for upper-class relations behind
the lathes   stamping machines   greasy smiles
missing fingers   under the bonnet   topping up
screwing tight   Saturday mornings time and a half
double on the day of some Lord   till the jobs
went walking out the plants into open spaces
wide enough to fit the blankness of a well-hung
face buried side by side   on top   beneath   whole
cartels   old folk hotels   see the odd one serving
tools slowly down the aisles   D.I.Y. you D.I.E.
that see you still get up early to make a cup of tea
for the wife long since gone   see for yourself
an empty barstool   pool cue in the rack
they sit in their mindful altar of past ambition
where every old man gets his last breath done.

The last old man

lies in a state surrounded by his near and far.
Top of his head exposed, strands of hair
lie lengthways across his wife's pillow. Alive, he stood
in front of the hallway mirror stiff as a tombstone
fingering Brylcreem bounce through black hair
making it shine like an oil spill. Day after day his face
saw the same head of hair in retreat   lashed ever-
decreasing strands over the bone of his skull
as his wife and daughters stood in the dark hall
watching in silence. Today she comes to prepare
his passing   strokes his face lifts his loyal hairs
laying them in her palm like an ancient artefact.
Chops off the final strands   deep against the roots.

House Rules

it's all about the taking part
it's all about the winning
start to finish fifty
goose-bumped bodies
amidst puberty's clump
freezing to sweating
running for your House
across the many fields
between cows and horses
leaping stile upon stile
past the cemetery
the cobblestoned hill
fully blown lungs
aware of the feat
parents' cry, go on
Charlie, faster Guy
head down, sharp elbows
at acutest of angles
giving you some space
through the icy brook
another's shoe stuck
in a pat, there's just three
in front now, all from
a different House
bottom of the hill
that ends in the sky
filling up on air
front foot bounce
between mole mounds
careful the weakened knee.
Dad's at the top, you know
not to stop, long slope home
skirting the farmhouse
through the final stream
the end a fifty yard rush
you break the hush
of coats & brollies
leaving the rest for dead
the only race you won.

Notes

The Fall is a poem after a film by Jonathan Glazer.

Home-Father Hydraulics: Immanuel Kant held that moral education is hydraulic: shame squashes down our vices, making space for virtue to rise up.

Swimming Away in Circles is loosely based on an Institute of Psychiatry research project I was involved in on the North Peckham Estate in the late 1990s.

the length of a lie > the length of a truth: a research study in the late noughties found that it took 30 percent longer to tell a lie than a truth.

Acknowledgements

A big thank you to the editors of the following publications where some of the poems have appeared:

And Other Poems (Josephine Corcoran), *Atrium* (Holly Magill/ Claire Walker), *The Brown Envelope Anthology* (Alan Morrison/ Kate J-R), *The Butcher's Dog* (Jo Clement, Emily Brenchi, Hannah Hodgson), *Cry of the Poor Anthology* (Fran Lock), *Culture Matters* (Mike Quille), *Fly on the Wall Press* (Isabelle Kenyon), *14 Magazine* (Richard Skinner), *Good Dadhood* (Sharon Larkin), *Poetry Salzburg* (Wolfgang Görtschacher), *Poetry Scotland* (Andy Jackson and Judy Taylor), *Red Poets Anthology* (Mike Jenkins), *the North* (Ann and Peter Sansom), *the Rialto* (Michael Mackmin), *Twin Skies Poems from Cork and Coventry Anthology* (Paul Casey, Raef Boylan), *Under the Radar* (Jane Commane/Matt Merritt), *Verve Poetry Press Anthology 84* (Helen Calcutt/Stuart Bartholomew).

Thanks also to the following people who have helped shape the collection and support my poetry more generally:

Jacqueline Saphra who helped give an early version of the manuscript shape, direction, and love.

My poetry brother Richard Skinner, with whom I toured in 2018. Mike Quille of Culture Matters who published *The Combination: a poetic coupling of the Communist Manifesto,* and Andy Croft of Smokestack Books, who published my first book *Precarious.* Both have been the main publishers of working class poetry for many years.

Malika Booker, who dispelled all the myths about poetry. Jill Abram, Director of Malika's Kitchen who supported my work for a number of years, as well as the rest of the members.

Thanks also to Brian Harrison, Monica Germana, Matthew Morrison, from the University of Westminster, where all this creative writing malarkey began.

Thank you to the Society of Authors, for providing a house for a Nine Arches writing retreat at Hartsop, Cumbria and to my fellow Nine Arches poets who were there; Jo Bell (my original mentor), Josephine Corcoran, Gregory Leadbetter, and Roy MacFarlane. It was a great week and I miss the walks, late night discussions, the whisky, and apple crumble.

Thank you to my publisher, and fellow Coventrian Jane Commane, who has supported my poetry long before agreeing to publish this collection. Thanks also to Angela Hicken of Nine Arches Press for her indefatigable support.

To my family: my wife, two sons, sister, brother-in-law, niece and nephew, my parents, and the in-laws.

Finally, many thanks to the old guard of the Cedars Pub and beyond, with whom I had the greatest time in my twenties in Coventry (despite Thatcher), then after in London, giving me values I carry with me today: Gordy, Paddy, Macca, Jules, Clare, Simon, Mark, Ben, Justine, Steve, Gemma, Jonney P, Mick K (RIP), Dave K, Silly Pete & Sue, Brads, CJ, Deace (John & Ray), Dal Boy, Spike, Stevo (Gez, Bren, Mick), Steve Owen (aka Eddie), Melv, Westy & Ange, Docko, Murph, Dicko, Stegga & Maria, Eddie, Reedy (Gez), Rudds (Sean, Martin), Raff, Willow, Bamb, Timmy (RIP), the Under 5s (Bren, Fal, Taff, Sprodge, Quirky, Goffy), and the older 'Bikers'. This book is for all of them.

HOUSE OF TOMORROW

Claire Lorrimer

C

CENTURY

LONDON   MELBOURNE   AUCKLAND   JOHANNESBURG

First published in Great Britain in 1987 by
Century Hutchinson Ltd
Brookmount House, 62–65 Chandos Place
London WC2N 4NW

Century Hutchinson South Africa (Pty) Ltd
PO Box 337, Bergvlei, 2012 South Africa

Century Hutchinson Australia Pty Ltd
PO Box 496, 16–22 Church Street, Hawthorn
Victoria 3122, Australia

Century Hutchinson New Zealand Ltd
PO Box 40–086, Glenfield, Auckland 10
New Zealand

British Library Cataloguing in Publication Data

Lorrimer, Claire
    House of tomorrow.
    1. Children—Institutional care—Great
    Britain
    Rn: Patricia Denise Clark   I. Title
    362.7′092′4   HV1146

ISBN 0-7126-1153-3

Printed in Great Britain by
Anchor Brendon Ltd,
Tiptree, Essex